COMPUTERS FOR KIDS

IBM PC EDITION

With special thanks to Corey Sandler for translating this book for use
with the IBM PC

COMPUTERS FOR KIDS

IBM PC EDITION

SALLY GREENWOOD LARSEN

creative computing press, morris plains, n.j.

Library of Congress Number: 83-72051
ISBN: 0-916688-56-9

Printed in the United States of America.

10 9 8 7 6 5 4 3 2 1

Creative Computing Press
39 E. Hanover Avenue
Morris Plains, New Jersey 07950

For Mary, With Love

TABLE OF CONTENTS

SECTION

SECTION 1: What is a Computer?

When cavemen and women had work to do, they had no machines or tools to help them. They had to do it all by themselves. Men and women have since invented many tools to help them with their work.

Instead of pounding with hands, we now use a hammer. The hammer lets us pound harder and longer than with hands alone.

The telescope was invented so that we could see farther into space. We can now see stars we did not know existed before we had the telescope to help our eyes.

Using our brains, we can remember information and solve problems. But there was a need for a tool that would extend the use of our brains, so the COMPUTER was invented.

Just as a hammer cannot do work without a person to hold it, a computer cannot work without a person to run it and tell it what to do. This person is called a PROGRAMMER.

Even the best hammer cannot do all the different things our hands can do. And even the best computer cannot do **everything** our brains can do.

A computer cannot feel emotion. It cannot feel happy or sad, as we can. A computer cannot combine two ideas together and take the best parts of each one to make a brand new idea all by itself.

But . . . a computer **can** do some of the simpler jobs our brains can do. And it can do some of them even faster than we can! A computer can remember many more things than most of us can with just our brains, especially things like long lists of names or numbers. This information is kept inside the computer in the MEMORY. Computer programmers call this information DATA.

A computer can **compare** data to see if one thing is bigger than another, or smaller, or the same. It can also put things in order.

A computer can sort many pieces of data and put together the things that are alike.

2

And a computer can look in its memory to find the data a programmer wants, and print out that data on a video screen or on a sheet of paper.

This book is about the IBM PC computer, made by IBM. These are special instructions for **this** computer. They will not work on all other kinds of computers.

The IBM PC is called a MICRO COMPUTER, because it is so small. Many businesses and universities have computers too, but theirs have many more jobs than our PC, so they are sometimes much larger. The biggest computers fill an entire room!

The IBM PC speaks a special computer language called BASIC. It is an easy language to learn, because it uses words like those we hear every day. Some other languages are called LOGO or COBOL or FORTRAN. You might hear about other languages when you find out more about computers.

3

SECTION 2: Flowcharting

When you want the computer to do a job for you, you must break down the job into small steps, so the computer can understand what to do. One big job may have many small steps, and sometimes it is hard to keep track of all the steps.

One way of keeping track is with a **flowchart**. A flowchart shows all the steps in a problem, shows what choices there are, and in what order the steps must be done.

On the next page is a flowchart showing all the little steps in a funny problem. The directions on this flowchart are things for you to do. They are not directions for the computer.

The shapes drawn around the steps show what **kind** of a step it is:

OVAL — for START or END.

RECTANGLE — for statements telling exactly what to do (you have no choice).

DIAMOND — for yes or no questions.

4

How to Scare Your Mom with an Elephant

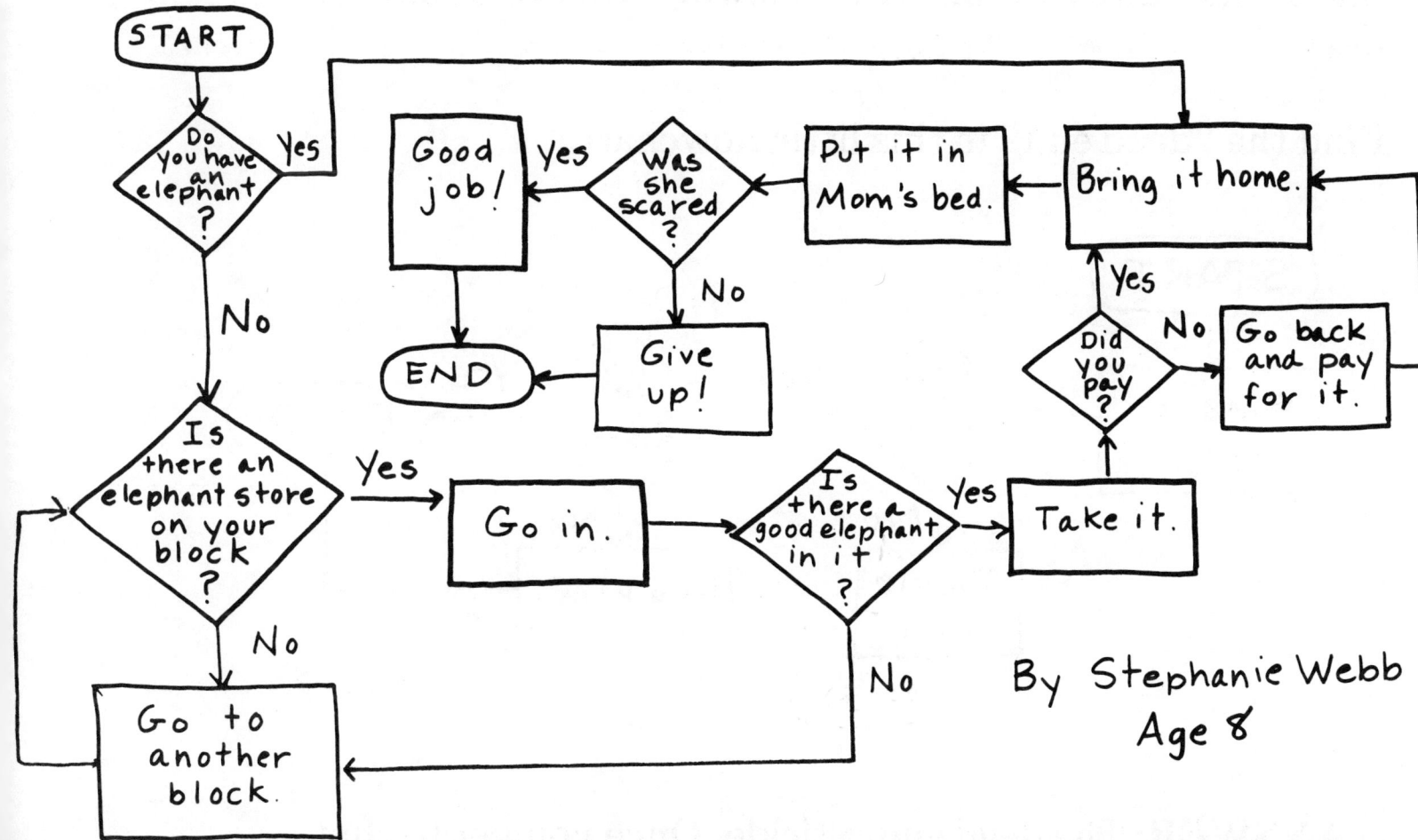

START

Do you have an elephant? → Yes

No ↓

Good job! ← Yes ← Was she scared? ← Put it in Mom's bed. ← Bring it home.

Was she scared? → No → Give up!

Good job! → END

Give up! → END

Is there an elephant store on your block? → Yes → Go in. → Is there a good elephant in it? → Yes → Take it.

No ↓

Is there a good elephant in it? → No

Take it. → Did you pay?

Did you pay? → Yes → Bring it home.

Did you pay? → No → Go back and pay for it.

No → Go to another block.

By Stephanie Webb
Age 8

The arrows on a flowchart show you what to do next. One arrow shows what to do if the answer is *yes*. The other arrow is for *no*.

5

There must be no "dead ends" in a flowchart. This means that there must always be an arrow showing what to do and where to go next.

Find the "dead end" in this little flowchart:

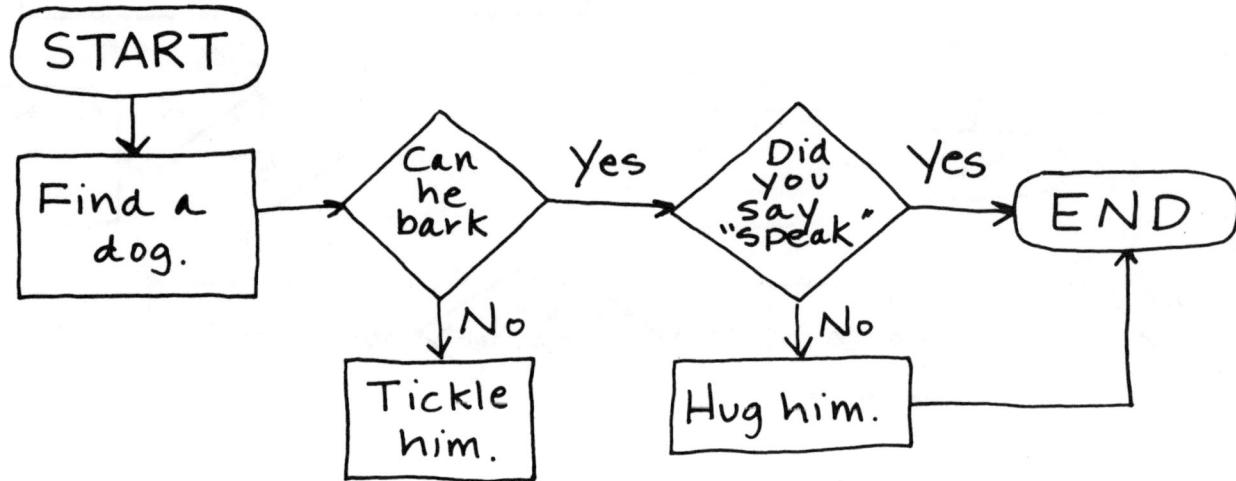

```
        ┌─────────┐
        │  START  │
        └────┬────┘
             │
             ▼
      ┌────────────┐         ╱╲          Yes       ╱╲          Yes    ┌───────┐
      │  Find a    │───────▶ Can ──────────────▶ Did you ──────────▶ │  END  │
      │  dog.      │         he                   say                └───────┘
      └────────────┘         bark                "speak"                  ▲
                              │                     │                     │
                              │ No                  │ No                  │
                              ▼                     ▼                     │
                         ┌────────┐          ┌───────────┐               │
                         │ Tickle │          │ Hug him.  │───────────────┘
                         │ him.   │          └───────────┘
                         └────────┘
```

ANSWER: The dead end is tickle him . Once you get to that

statement, there is no arrow showing you where to go next.

When you write your own practice flowcharts, pick a subject you know something about. Also, your flowchart will be much more interesting if you pick a topic which has some choices in it. You want both questions *and* statements in your flowchart—not just a page full of one statement after another. Here are some suggestions:

1. How to make a peanut butter and jelly sandwich.

2. How to take a bath.

3. How to make your mother scream.

4. How to play kickball.

5. How to buy a birthday present.

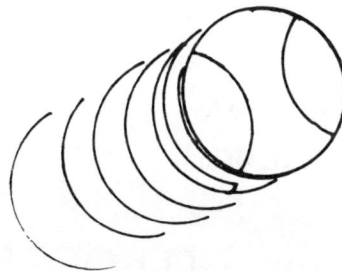

Here is an example:

(I have drawn only **part** of this flowchart.)

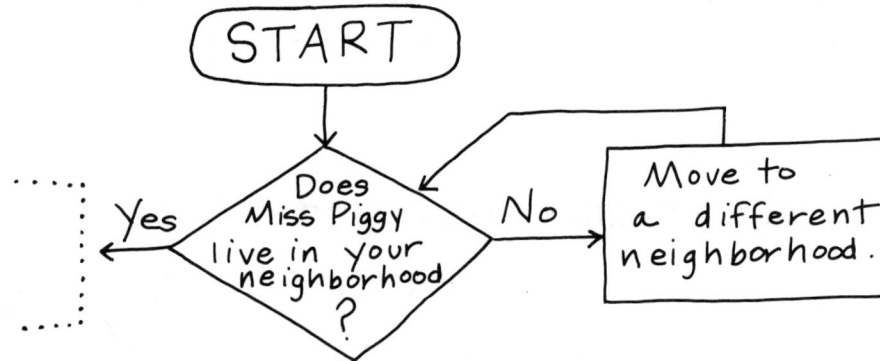

If you follow the directions for this part of the flowchart, you will keep moving to a new neighborhood until you are living in Miss Piggy's neighborhood.

This is called a **DO-LOOP.**

In a DO-LOOP, you keep coming back to the question you asked until you finally get the answer you need so you can go on to the rest of the flowchart.

In this example, in order to "meet Miss Piggy," you had to first move into her neighborhood.

We will learn more about DO-LOOPS in Section 6. In the next sections, you will see how we use flowcharts to help us write our own computer programs.

8

SECTION 3:
Running the IBM PC Computer

The IBM PC has three basic parts:

The Keyboard - This looks like a regular typewriter keyboard, except that it has a lot of extra keys and numbers added on the left and right. A picture of the keyboard is shown below:

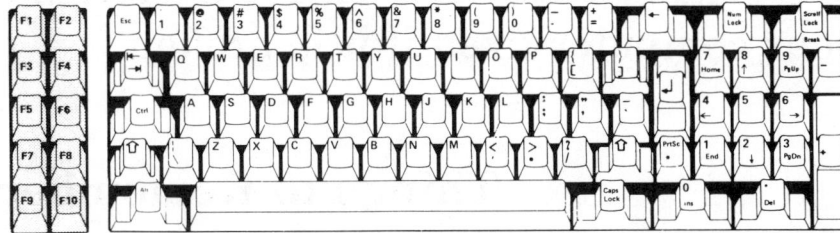

The Computer - This is the box which your keyboard plugs into. Inside are the electronic "chips" and "central processor." On the front are one or two "disk drives" where magnetic disks can play programs into or record information from your computer. We won't need disk drives to use this book.

The TV Screen - This is where you'll see the words and numbers you type on the keyboard. This is not a regular television set like the one you have at your house. It has no channels and sound. You can't watch TV programs on it.

9

The first time you use the IBM PC, have an adult help you set it up and show you where the on/off switch for the computer is. Some television screens have separate on/off switches, while others come on automatically when you turn on the computer.

It is not hard to set up the computer once you know how, but it is important that it is done correctly, or you could break it.

IF YOU AREN'T SURE — ASK FOR HELP! It could take weeks to get your computer fixed if it is broken.

Things to Remember

1. If you don't hear a "beep" from the computer within about a minute after you turn it on, the computer might not be working right. (You did check to see that it was plugged in, didn't you?)

2. If you don't see anything on your television screen, make sure that it is also plugged in and that its on/off switch is on.

3. Your computer's memory will only remember what is in it as long as the power is on. If you turn off the computer or unplug it, you will lose your program. (Turning off only the TV won't matter.)

10

4. Watch out for the electrical cords. You don't want to trip over them, and you don't want to kick them loose accidentally because then you'd lose your program.

5. Be gentle with the keyboard — don't pound on it, please!

6. Don't touch the front of the television screen, because you might smudge it.

7. Turn off the computer (and the TV if it has a separate on/off switch) when you're done.

What Happens When You Turn On Your Computer?

There are many, many different brands of computers being sold, and each is a little bit different. Some computers need to get instructions from a plug-in cartridge (like the ones in video games). Some computers need to get their instructions from a tape cassette (like the ones you might use in a tape recorder). Other computers need to get their instructions from a "disk," which is like a thin music record.

On your IBM PC, you can give instructions from a cassette or from a disk, but there's an even easier way. The IBM has built into it a beginning programming language called "BASIC" and that is all that we will need for this book.

Ask an adult to help you make sure there are no disks in the disk drives, and then turn on the electrical power to the computer.

SECTION 4: Getting Ready to Program

When you write a program, you are writing a list of instructions the computer needs to do a particular job, like printing your name on the screen. These instructions are called **program statements,** and you'll learn more about them in Section 5.

But sometimes you need to tell the machine itself to do something, such as get rid of an old program so you can write a new one, or clear all the printing off the TV screen. These are called **commands** — they are not part of the program.

You type them in and press the "ENTER" key and the computer does them right away. On the IBM PC, the "ENTER" key is near where your right pinkie should rest. It is a slightly larger key with an arrow with a little hook on it. It looks like this:

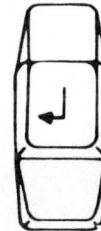

Program statements all have **line numbers** in front of them, to tell the computer which statement should be done first. (You will see these line numbers in Section 5.) Remember that commands do **not** have a line number because they are not part of a program.

Here are some of the **commands** you will need. Remember to press the "ENTER" key after each one you use.

| CLS | When you type this and press "ENTER" it takes all of the printing off the screen, but it does **not** take your program out of the memory. Remember, just because the information isn't printed on the TV screen doesn't mean it is no longer stored inside the computer's memory! We'll tell you later how to find out what the computer has in its memory. |

| KEY OFF | This can be a command or a statement, and it erases all of the numbers and instructions which appear on the bottom of your screen. You won't need them for this book. But just in case you want to bring them back, the command is KEY ON. |

| NEW | This erases your last program from the memory so you can start a new program with a "clean" memory. |

| LIST | This command prints out, in order, whatever program statements you have typed into the memory so far. |

14

RUN

This is the command that tells the computer you want it to begin **doing** the job you've given it the instructions for. This is called **executing** the program. When the computer is done with your job, it will print "Ok" on the screen.

CTRL-BREAK

If you want to stop the operation of a program or if your program is caught in an endless loop, you can tell the computer to stop by holding down the Ctrl (control) key, which is left of the letter A, and then typing the Scroll Lock/Break key, which is at the top right corner of the keyboard.

CONT

You can tell the computer to continue executing a program you've halted by typing in the word CONT (for continue) and hitting the ENTER key. The computer will pick up the program at the line number it was working on when it was interrupted. You cannot continue a program which was stopped because of an error, though. You'll have to fix the mistake first and then type and enter RUN.

SECTION 5: Print and Variables

Let's begin by writing a program using the PRINT statement. You should start your program with a KEY OFF statement and then a CLS statement:

```
5  KEY OFF

10 CLS
```

This clears the screen, to get rid of any "garbage" which might mess up your program later. Remember — CLS only clears the TV screen — it does not erase your program from the computer's memory. (CLS is one of the few commands that can be given a line number and become a program statement.)

Now we'll use a PRINT statement to print out your first message:

```
5  KEY OFF

10 CLS

15 PRINT "HELLO!  I AM YOUR IBM PC COMPUTER!"

20 PRINT "THIS MUST BE YOUR FIRST PROGRAM."

25 END
```

and the last line will be an END statement to show the computer where the program ENDs.

16

Have you typed that program on the keyboard and checked it on the television screen? Now type in RUN and then press the "ENTER" key (the key with the ⬅ symbol). This is what the computer will print on the screen:

You try typing it in.

Remember to press the "ENTER" key each time you finish typing a line.

RUN has no number in front of it.

See if your program turns out the same as the screen I've drawn here.

```
HELLO! I AM YOUR IBM PC COMPUTER!

THIS MUST BE YOUR FIRST PROGRAM

Ok
```

Where did that "Ok" come from? That's the computer's way of telling you it is finished executing your program and is ready to do something else.

Whenever you use a statement like PRINT "HELLO!", the computer will print out **exactly** what you put between the quotation marks. Even if what you put is silly! Even if it is spelled incorrectly.

17

Here are some examples for you to try. Then go ahead and make up some of your own!

```
NEW

5  KEY OFF

10 CLS

15 PRINT "I KIN SPELL REEL GOOD."

20 PRINT "GIGGLE! GIGGLE!"

25 END

RUN

NEW

5  KEY OFF

10 CLS

15 PRINT "MY NAME IS JOHN SMITH."

20 PRINT "MY NAME IS MARY JONES."

25 END

RUN

NEW

5 KEY OFF

10 CLS

15 PRINT "I AM A FRIENDLY COMPUTER."

20 END

RUN
```

(NEW and RUN are not part of the program, but I'm putting it here so you don't forget to type it in each time you want to run your program. Later, I won't write it down each time.)

18

Before we go on with PRINT statements, let's talk about **line numbers.**

Every statement in a program has a number in front of it. This tells the computer which statement to do first. The computer will start with the lowest number and end with the highest number, no matter how many numbers you skip in between. Good programmers always count by fives or tens when they number their lines, so that if they leave out a line by mistake, they can put it in later, and there will be room. For example:

```
5   KEY OFF

10  CLS

15  PRINT "MY NAME IS ROBBIE."        James

20  PRINT "MY BIRTHDAY IS JULY 3RD."   aug. 13th

25  END                               Print born 1975
                                       Print
30  on wenesday
35. Print I'm 9 years old
```

Now — if I wanted to put a line in my program telling how old Robbie is, right after line 15, I could just type in:

```
16 PRINT "I AM 9 YEARS OLD."
```

If I type in CLS (and the "ENTER" key) to clear the screen, and then type and enter LIST, the computer will put line 16 into the program in the right place and this is what will show up on the television screen:

```
5  KEY OFF

10 CLS

15 PRINT "MY NAME IS ROBBIE."

16 PRINT "I AM 9 YEARS OLD."

20 PRINT "MY BIRTHDAY IS JULY 3RD."

25 END
```

This is very helpful if you forget something in your program.

You can use the same idea to delete (take out) a line in your program, if you make a mistake or just decide you don't want that line anymore.

20

```
5  KEY OFF
10 CLS
15 PRINT "TODAY IS TOOSDAY."
20 END
```

In this program, line 15 has a spelling mistake. To get rid of line 15 completely, all you do is type in 15 and hit the return key. This will erase line 15 from the memory. Then you could type in a new line 15 in its place.

But suppose you are typing a line and you notice right away that you've made a mistake, even before you go on to the next line. Can you erase part of the line? Of course!

Look at the right side of the top of the keyboard. There you'll see the ← key. This key looks **almost** like the "ENTER" key, except that it is smaller, and does not have the little hook at the end. It looks like this:

This key is like the backspace key on a typewriter, only on the computer it erases everything it passes over. Remember that the ← key only works for the line you are typing on right then. If you are typing on line 15, you cannot erase something on line 5 with the ← key. The best way for you to correct a line you've already entered into the computer is to retype it (with the line number).

Remember

You may also be wondering why zero is written with a line through it, like this: Ø

This is done on all computers so there is no mix-up between the number zero and the letter O. You should use the special zero when you write your programs on paper, too.

When you type in your own programs on the IBM PC, if you type in something that the computer does not understand, the screen may display an **error message.** This means you have made a mistake and you should try again.

We've already seen how the PRINT statement can be used to print out words. The PRINT statement can also be used to skip a line.

```
5   KEY OFF

10  CLS

15  PRINT "HELLO"

20  PRINT

25  PRINT "GOODBYE"

30  END
```

```
HELLO


GOODBYE



Ok
```

22

Remember that you had to use the " mark around words you wanted the computer to print out. If you don't use the quotation marks in a PRINT statement, the IBM PC will work like a calculator.

```
5   KEY OFF

10  CLS

15  PRINT 10 + 20

20  END
```

```
30

OK
```

This program will print out the **answer** to 10+20, which is 30. If you wanted to print out the actual problem 10+20, you would write it like this: 15 PRINT "10 + 20"

Do you see the difference?

Here is a PRINT program and the results on the IBM PC screen when the program is executed. Look it over carefully.

```
5   KEY OFF

10  CLS

15  PRINT "RED"

20  PRINT "   BLUE"

25  PRINT "YELLOW"

30  PRINT "5 + 6"

35  PRINT 5 + 6

40  PRINT

45  PRINT "PINK PICKLES"

50  END
```

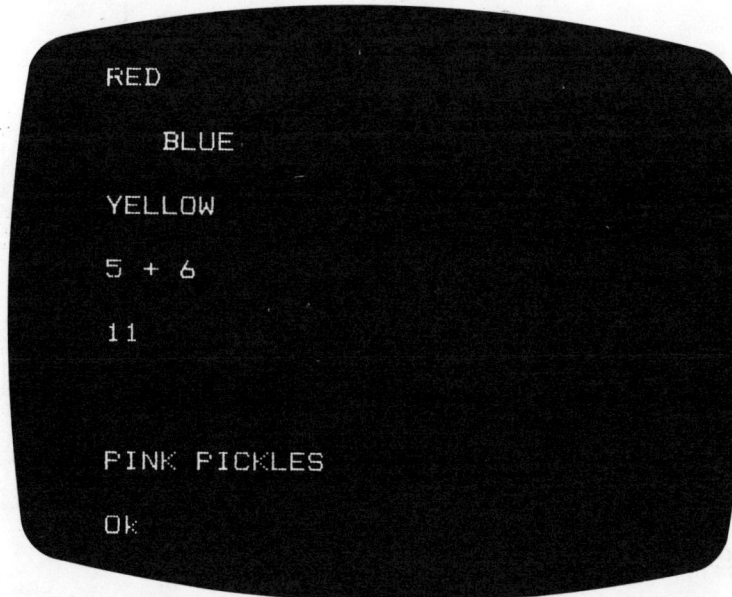

```
RED

       BLUE

YELLOW

5 + 6

11


PINK PICKLES

OK
```

23

Notice that line 50 END does **not** print the word "END" on the screen. It just tells the computer that this is the **end** of your program.

The computer can also keep a number in its memory, and print it out later when you ask for it. Let's look at how the memory works.

The memory is like a big Post Office, with letters of the alphabet on each "mailbox." You put a number in the "mailbox" by giving it a name, called a "variable," which can be done by using a LET statement.

A	B	C	D
5	7	2	0

```
5   KEY OFF
10  CLS
15  LET A = 5
20  LET B = 7
25  LET C = 2
30  LET D = 0
```

Now, in this program, whenever you use a statement like 35 PRINT A, the computer will print out on the television screen the number or value in the mailbox called "A". (When you write your own programs later, always be sure you have put a number in mailbox A before you ask the computer to print it out, or you will get an error.)

In computer programs, the letter names you give to the "mailboxes" are called variables. If you write a statement like 15 PRINT A + B the computer will look in A to see what that value is, then find the value for B, and then add them together and print out just the answer for you. Here is an example:

```
5   KEY OFF
10  CLS
15  LET A = 6
20  LET B = 4
25  PRINT A + B
30  END
```

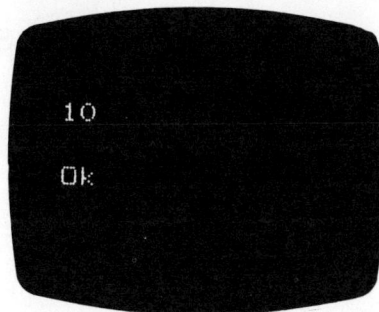

```
10

Ok
```

MEMORY

A	B
6	4

If you want to change the number stored in mailbox A, you can use another LET statement later in your program. This will erase the old value for A and put in the new value.

NOTE: The IBM-PC and most other computers use a few special symbols for arithmetic.

Addition	+	3 plus 4 is written as 3 + 4
Subtraction	–	5 minus 2 is written as 5 – 2
Multiplication	*	6 times 8 is written as 6 * 8
Division	/	6 divided by 2 is written as 6/2

There are two other symbols you may want to use later:

| Less than | < | 3 is less than 6 is written as 3 < 6 |
| More than | > | 6 is more than 3 is written as 6 > 3 |

SECTION 6: GOTO, INPUT, and RND

PRINT statements alone don't make very exciting programs, but this section has three new statements which make programming more fun!

Let's look at each one, then write some simple programs.

GOTO tells the computer to **go to** the line number listed, and do what it says there.

```
5   KEY OFF

10  CLS

15  PRINT "HELLO"

20  GOTO 15

25  END
```

Every time the computer gets to line 20, the program tells it to go to line 15.

This program prints "HELLO" over and over and over again, without stopping. It would go on all night long, if you didn't stop it. This is called an "endless loop."

To stop an endless loop on the IBM PC, you must "break" the program. Look on the left side of the keyboard for the small key marked "Ctrl". This is the "control" key, and it acts like a special shift key on the IBM PC. Now look across the keyboard to the very top on the right side and you'll see a key marked "Scroll Lock" on top, and "Break" on the front. Hold down "Ctrl" and then type the "Scroll Lock/Break" key to break the endless loop.

26

Now we'll look at the INPUT statement. INPUT asks you to type in (put in) a number while the program is running.

```
5   KEY OFF

10  CLS

20  PRINT "TYPE IN YOUR AGE"

25  INPUT A
```

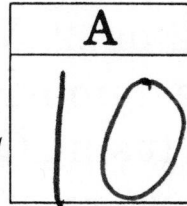

This sets up a memory space called A, and when you type in your age, it will be stored in memory space A.

Now we can use that information:

```
30  PRINT "YOUR AGE IS "

35  PRINT A

40  END
```

What would have happened if you had typed PRINT "A"?

Type in this program on the computer and try it yourself. You will notice that when the computer reaches an INPUT statement, while it is running a program, it will stop and print "?" and wait for your answer.

When you write your own INPUT programs, you must always be careful to PRINT a statement to tell the person who uses your program what the computer is asking them.

27

RND (which is short for Random) also stores a number in the memory, but this time the **computer** picks the number! When your IBM PC sees the RND statement, it picks a number between 0 and 1, like .1234 or .5692 or .2. We're going to do two things to our program to make the numbers easier: first, we're going to ask the computer to multiply (using the ∗) the RND number by 100 to make it larger than 1, and we're going to add another statement which tells the computer to "round" the number up to a whole number (called an "integer").

```
5   KEY OFF

10  CLS

15  DEFINT X

20  LET X = RND * 100

25  PRINT X

30  END
```

Line 15 tells the computer to **DEF**ine as an **INT**eger the variable X.

Line 20 makes X equal to RND (the random number) and then multiplies it by 100. The number is then stored in memory space X.

You'll find RND to be a very handy statement for game programs. After we learn about IF-THEN statements in Section 7, you will be able to write your own computer game of "Guess my number!"

28

SECTION 7: IF-THEN and FOR-NEXT

FOR-NEXT statements are lots of fun, because you can make the computer do all kinds of work for you!

```
5 KEY OFF

10 CLS

15 FOR X = 1 to 5

20 PRINT "TOM"

25 NEXT X

30 PRINT "I'M DONE"

35 END
```

This statement says, "I'm going to do something 5 times."

What it will do is print "TOM." This statement tells it what to do each time.

This statement is the "counter." It counts how many times the computer has done its job. When it has done the job the right number of times, it will go on to the next line of directions.

This part of the program is called a FOR-NEXT LOOP, because the computer "loops" through that part of the program over and over again, until it has done its job the right number of times.

29

We can also write a program which has several lines between the FOR and NEXT statements in the loop:

FOR-NEXT LOOP

```
 5  KEY OFF

10 CLS

15 FOR X = 1 TO 5

20 PRINT "MY NAME IS JANICE KEEFE."

25 PRINT "I LIKE TO WRITE PROGRAMS."

30 PRINT "I HAVE MY OWN COMPUTER."

35 NEXT X

40 END
```

This program will write all three of the PRINT statements each time, until it has gone through the loop five times. It will print a total of 15 lines.

You may use any variable you wish in a FOR-NEXT loop, but the variable must be the **same** in both statements, or the computer will give you an error message:

```
10 FOR Q = 1 TO 12

15 PRINT "HARRY"

20 NEXT Q
```

These two variables must be the same.

This program will print "HARRY" 12 times.

Here are a few sample problems to try. Now take some time and write your own!

Name

```
5   KEY OFF

10  CLS

15  FOR Z = 1 TO 100

20  PRINT "SUSAN IS GREAT."

25  NEXT Z

30  END
```

Numbers

```
5   KEY OFF

10  CLS

15  FOR R = 1 TO 100

20  PRINT R

25  NEXT R

30  END
```

I have given names to these programs to make them easier to remember. Don't type in the name as part of the program, or the computer will give you an error message.

IF-THEN statements provide a "test" for your programs.

```
5   KEY OFF

10  CLS

15  PRINT "TYPE IN YOUR FAVORITE

    NUMBER"

20  INPUT N

25  IF N = 5 THEN PRINT "YOU HAVE

    PICKED THE LUCKY NUMBER!"

30  END
```

This statement looks in "mailbox" N to see what number is stored there in the memory. If it is 5, then the computer is told to PRINT "YOU HAVE PICKED THE LUCKY NUMBER!" If the number is not 5 (if the number "fails" the test), then the computer ignores the rest of the statement and goes on to the next line.

Let's think about how IF-THEN statements work.

Pretend you are "inside" your program, and you are following all the instructions in the program, just as the computer would. You are going down the road, and you come to a fork, where there are two ways to go. (This is the IF-THEN statement in the program you are following.)

to THEN

Mr. IF

Mr. IF has a "test" for you. If you pass the test, you may go down the fork in the road marked THEN. If you do not pass the test, you must go the other way.

An IF-THEN statement is called a **branch** in your program.

We can also show this with a flowchart:

```
5   KEY OFF
10  CLS
15  PRINT "TYPE IN YOUR FAVORITE NUMBER."
20  INPUT N
25  IF N = 5 THEN PRINT "YOU PICKED THE LUCKY NUMBER!"
30  END
```

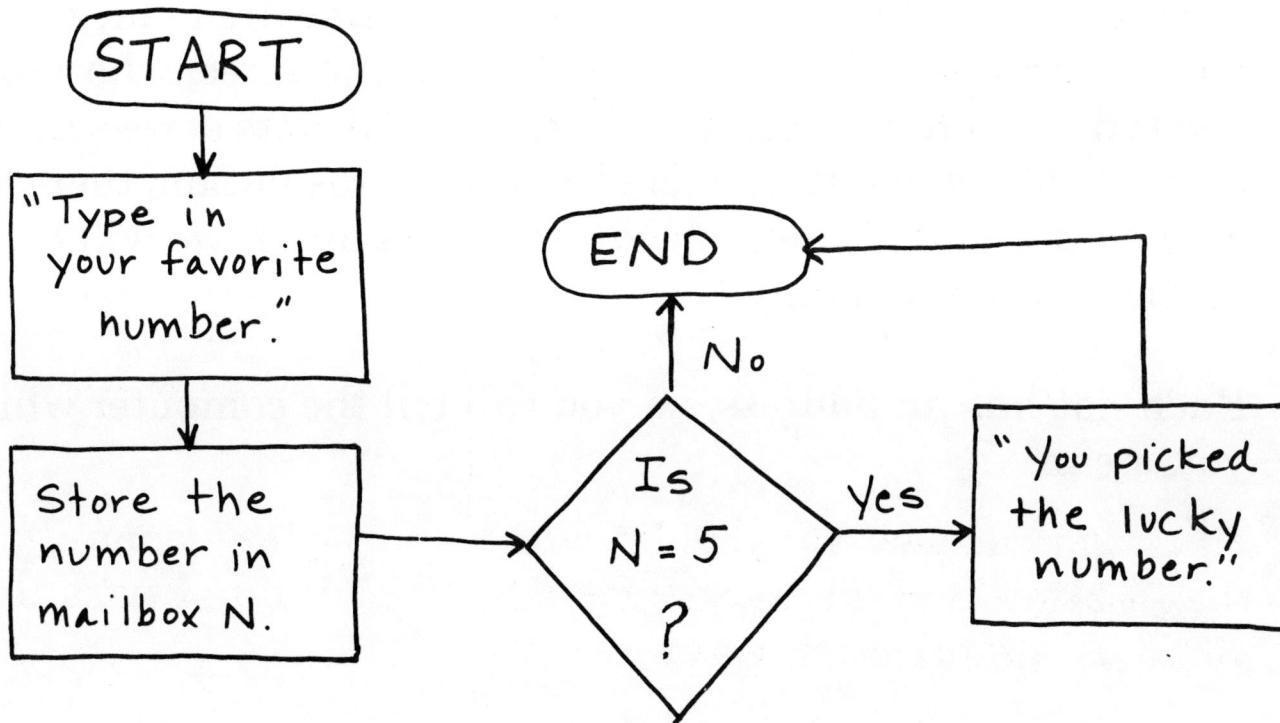

33

SECTION 8: Graphics Programs

Graphics programs let you make pictures on the screen with dots of light. In order to run the programs in this chapter, you'll need to have the Graphics Adapter installed in your IBM PC. If you don't know if this adapter is installed, ask an adult to help you check.

There are two types of graphics which can be displayed on a television screen attached to your IBM PC — "medium resolution" and "high resolution." If you look very carefully at the words and numbers on the screen, you can see that they are made up of little dots. High resolution has more dots on the screen than medium resolution. In high resolution, there are 640 dots across the screen and 200 dots down the screen. In medium resolution, there are 320 dots across and 200 dots down. In this chapter, we will deal with medium resolution only.

Each dot has an address, so you can tell the computer which dot you mean.

Here is a picture of part of the screen. Each of the black dots has an address made up of two numbers.

To get the first number, you count how far **across** the screen that dot is.

The second number shows how far **down** from the top of the screen that dot is.

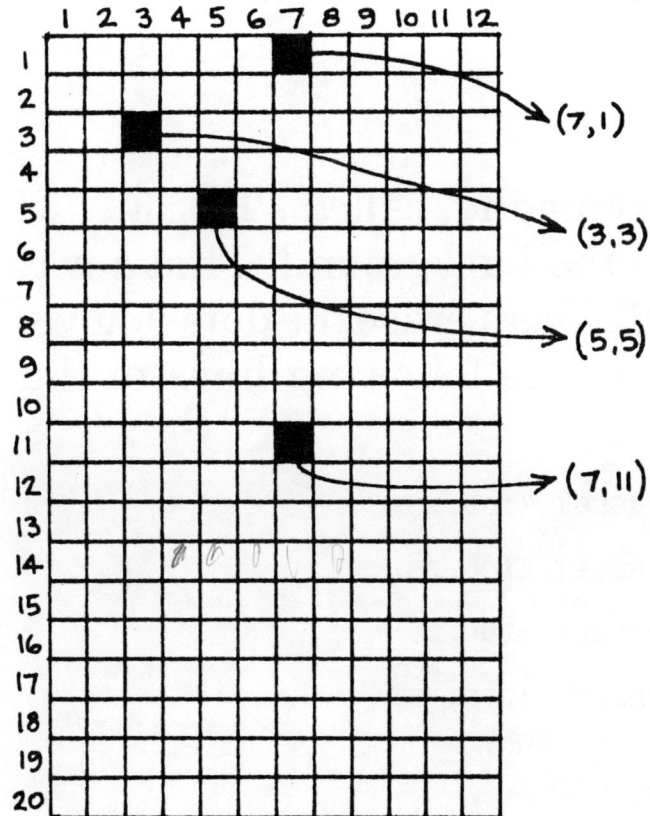

35

To light up a dot at an address, you use a PSET statement.

```
5   CLS

10  KEY OFF

15  SCREEN 1,1

20  PSET  (100,25)

25  PSET  (100,75)

30  PSET  (200,25)

35  PSET  (200,75)

40  END
```

This statement tells the computer you want medium resolution. You can try SCREEN 2 if you'd like to experiment with high resolution.

There's another command, called PRESET, which draws dots in the same color as the background. That's a complicated way of saying that PRESET can erase the dots you've drawn with PSET. To try this out, add the following lines to the program you just ran:

```
36  PRESET  (100,25)

37  PRESET  (100,75)

38  PRESET  (200,25)

39  PRESET  (200,75)
```

36

A special note: When you write your own graphics programs, try not to make all your dots in the upper left corner of the screen. When your program is over and Ok comes on the screen, it may erase them.

When you count out the address for a dot, we call the number **across** the screen "X". This is the first letter in the address:

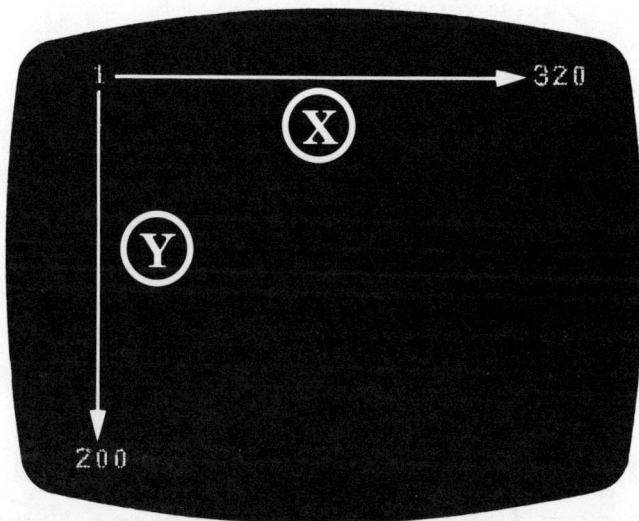

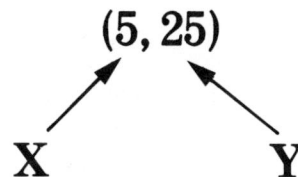

(5, 25)

X   Y

We call the number counted **down** from the top of the screen "Y". This is the second letter (or number) in the address.

We need to know about these variables used to name points, because often you will want to write an address in a PSET statement as (X, Y) so you can change X and Y easily.

This may sound confusing, but it's not once you try it. Here's an example to get you started:

Rain

```
5   CLS

10  KEY OFF

15  SCREEN 1,1

20  LET X = 1

25  LET Y = 1

30  PSET (X,Y)

35  X = X + 1

40  Y = Y + 1

45  IF X < 200 GOTO 30

50  END
```

These statements increase these variables by one.

This statement tells the computer to stop drawing the line when it reaches the 200 limit for the bottom of the screen.

Writing a graphics program only with PSET statements that have an address for one single point can take a very long time because every single dot needs a line of its own.

Using (X, Y) as an address makes the job much easier. Let's look at a way to draw lines using (X, Y) and FOR-NEXT loops.

38

Vertical Line

```
5  CLS

10 KEY OFF

15 SCREEN 1,1

20 FOR Y = 1 TO 150

25 PSET (50,Y)

35 NEXT Y

40 END
```

The values of Y will go from 1 to 150 (down the screen).

This line will be drawn at 50 spaces across the screen.

Why don't you see what happens if you were to add a line like this one: 30 PSET (100, Y)

Horizontal Line

```
5  CLS

10 KEY OFF

15 SCREEN 1,1

20 FOR X = 1 TO 150

25 PSET (X,48)

35 NEXT X

40 END
```

The values of X will go from 1 to 150 (across the screen).

This line will be drawn at 48 spaces down.

Try adding a line: 30 PSET (X, 96)

39

Putting It All Together

If you remove some of the repeating statements from the two earlier programs, you could join them together, like this:

```
5   CLS
10  KEY OFF
15  SCREEN 1,1
20  FOR Y = 1 TO 150
25  PSET (50,Y)
30  PSET (100,Y)
35  NEXT Y
40  FOR X = 1 TO 150
45  PSET (X,48)
50  PSET (X,96)
55  END
```

SECTION 9: Sample Programs

Rain

```
5   CLS

10  KEY OFF

15  SCREEN 1,1

20  LET X = 1

25  LET Y = 1

30  PSET (X,Y)

35  X = X + 1

40  Y = Y + 1

45  IF X < 200 GOTO 30

50  END
```

Worm Race

```
5   CLS

10  KEY OFF

15  SCREEN 1,1

20  FOR X = 1 TO 320

25  PSET (X, 24)

30  PSET (X,48)

35  NEXT X

40  END
```

Stars

```
5 CLS

10 KEY OFF

15 SCREEN 1,1

20 DEFINT X,Y

25 LET X = RND * 320

30 LET Y = RND * 200

35 PSET (X,Y)

40 GOTO 25

45 END
```

Defines X and Y as INTEGERS (whole numbers).

Lines 25 and 30 assign random numbers to X and Y that are within the 320 across by 200 down dot pattern of your TV in Medium Resolution.

Computer Panic

```
5 CLS

10 KEY OFF

15 PRINT "HELP! THIS COMPUTER IS CRAZY!"

20 GOTO 5
```

Note: **Stars** and **Computer Panic** contain endless loops. To stop them, you'll need to type the CTRL-Scroll Lock/Break combination. Could you write instructions which would stop these programs from running after they've printed a certain number of times? You might try a FOR-NEXT and IF-THEN test.

42

Here's a program which uses the characters on the keyboard to draw a picture. Can you make your own pictures, too?

Pine Tree

```
5  CLS

10 KEY OFF

20 PRINT "        X"

25 PRINT "       XXX"

30 PRINT "      XXXXX"

35 PRINT "     XXXXXXX"

40 PRINT "    XXXXXXXXX"

45 PRINT "XXXXXXXXXXX"

50 PRINT "        X"

55 PRINT "        X"

60 PRINT "        X"

65 END
```

Would you like to make your tree sparkle? Try changing Line 65 to: 65 GOTO 5. The program will go back to the top CLS and then draw the tree all over again. How will you stop the program?

Guess My Number

```
5   CLS

10  KEY OFF

15  DEFINT N,G

20  LET N = RND * 100

25  PRINT "I HAVE A SECRET NUMBER."

30  PRINT

35  PRINT "IT IS BETWEEN 1 AND 100."

40  PRINT "PLEASE TYPE IN YOUR GUESS:"

45  INPUT G

50  IF N = G THEN PRINT "CONGRATULATIONS! YOU WIN!"

55  IF N = G THEN END

60  IF N > G THEN PRINT "TRY A HIGHER NUMBER."

65  IF N < G THEN PRINT "TRY A LOWER NUMBER."

70  GOTO 40

75  END
```

44

SECTION 10: Glossary of Statements and Commands

BEEP   Makes the computer "beep." Try adding a statement just before the END statement of one of your programs, like: 74 BEEP

CLS   Clears any writing or graphics off the screen (but does not erase the program from memory).

CONT   Continues the execution of a program after you stop it by using CTRL-BREAK.

CTRL-BREAK   Stops the execution of a program. You must hold down the Ctrl key (left of the letter A) and then type the Scroll Lock/Break key (at the top right corner of the keyboard).

DEFINT   DEFine a variable as an INTeger (a whole number). If you use a statement like 20 DEFINT X, you are telling the computer to treat X as a whole number only.

END   tells the computer the program is over.

45

ENTER	this key must be pressed each time you finish typing a line. The ENTER key is on the right side of the keyboard.
FOR-NEXT	a type of do-loop which has the computer perform some action a certain number of times.

Example:
```
10 FOR X = 1 TO 100
15 PRINT "HELLO"
20 NEXT X
```

GOTO	tells the computer to skip to a certain line number in the program.
IF-THEN	a type of branch statement which puts a "test" in the program. If the test is passed, the computer will follow special instructions you give it.
INPUT	types out a question mark when the program is executed, and waits for an answer to be typed in. The answer is stored in a certain memory space.

Example:
```
15 PRINT "TYPE IN YOUR AGE"
20 INPUT N
```

46

INTEGER   a whole number. The computer will round a variable with a value like 2.748 up to 3 if you tell it to. See DEFINT.

LET   assigns a number to a memory space (or variable).

Example: `15 LET R = 100`

LIST   prints out on the screen a list, in order, of the program statements you have typed into the memory.

NEW   erases the old program from the memory.

PRINT   tells the computer you want it to write something on the screen.

PSET   lights up a certain dot on the screen.

Example: 15 PSET (110, 35) lights up the dot at 110 spaces over and 35 spaces down. PRESET draws a dot in the background color, erasing a dot you've drawn with PSET.

47

RUN   starts the execution of the program. This command is **not** part of the program itself, and it does not have a line number.

RND   has the computer pick a number at random. The number will be between 0 and 1, like .2573. If you want a larger number, tell the computer you want the variable multiplied by a certain value. If you want only whole numbers, put in a DEFINT statement.

Example:
```
15 DEFINT X
20 X = RND * 100
```

SCREEN 1, 1   tells your IBM PC that you want graphics drawn in Medium Resolution, which is 320 dots across the screen and 200 dots down. SCREEN 2 tells your computer you want High Resolution, which is 640 dots across and 200 dots down.

48

Simulate these computer runs. Show your "printout" on the screen.

```
5   CLS
10  KEY OFF
15  PRINT "BIG"
20  PRINT
25  PRINT "YELLOW"
30  PRINT "BLUE"
35  END
```

```
5   CLS
10  KEY OFF
15  PRINT "THE ANSWER"
20  PRINT 30 * 2
25  PRINT 30 + 2
30  PRINT 30 - 2
35  PRINT "THE END"
40  END
```

49

NAME *James Barber*

Here is a program and "printout." Find and fix the mistake in the program so a run will produce what is shown on the screen.

```
10 CLS
15 KEY OFF
20 PRINT 20 + 6
30 PRINT 30 + 4
35 PRINT
40 PRINT "60 - 3"
45 PRINT 10 - 10
50 PRINT "HELLO"
55 END
```

```
26


24


57
```

50

NAME _James Barber_

Write a program to print out the dots shown below. Don't forget the END statement!

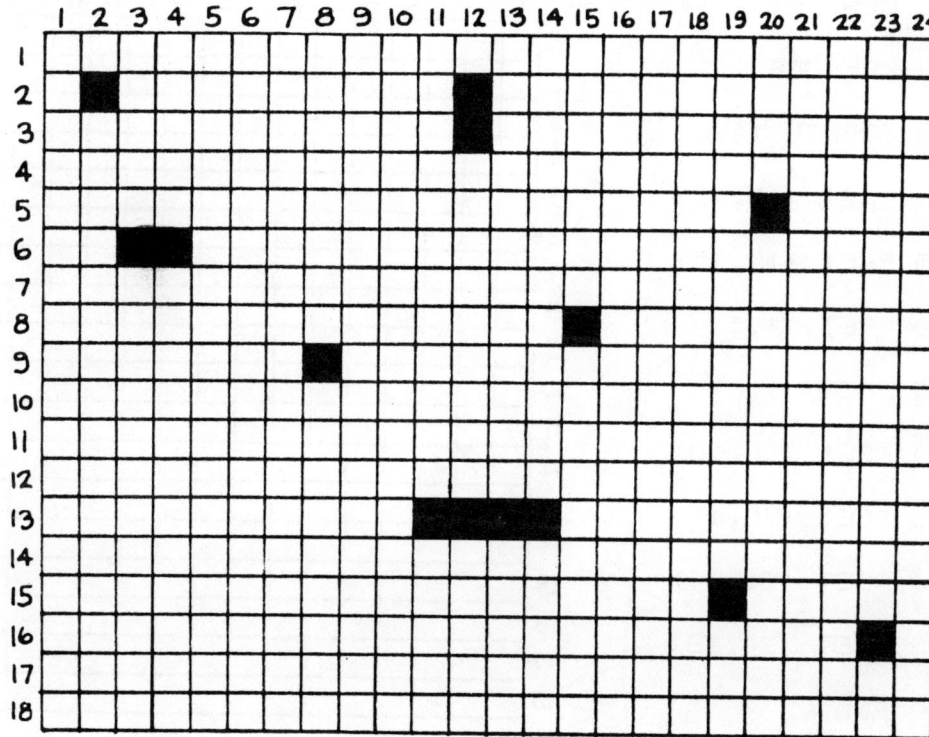

	1	2	3	4	5	6	7	8	9	10	11	12	13	14	15	16	17	18	19	20	21	22	23	24
1																								
2		■										■												
3												■												
4																								
5																				■				
6			■	■																				
7																								
8															■									
9								■																
10																								
11																								
12																								
13											■	■	■	■										
14																								
15																			■					
16																						■		
17																								
18																								

51

On the graph below, color in each dot which will light up when you run this program:

RUN

```
5  CLS

10 KEY OFF

15 SCREEN 1,1

20 PSET (15,12)

25 PSET (12,15)

30 PSET (1,5)

35 PSET (1,6)

40 PSET (10,10)

45 PSET (20,14)

50 PSET (21,14)

55 PSET (24,18)

60 END
```

52

Notes for Teachers and Parents

I am not, by any stretch of the imagination, a sophisticated programmer. I took one programming course in college, and have spent many years working with elementary school children. I've taught microcomputing programming to nearly 300 children, ranging in age from 4 to 12, and have yet to run into any children who aren't dying to get their hands on the keyboard. Computers are a natural — they give immediate feedback, and allow children to create something all their own. I love teaching programming. It is one of the most exciting things I've ever done.

Candidates for teaching programming to young children must have one trait above all others — the ability to interact with the children on a peer level, and learn along with them. Computer programming is not just a skill — it is a tool. You learn programming not as a study in itself, but because of what you can accomplish with it. In any one computer program, there are many ways to approach and solve the problem at hand. The thing I say most often to my students is, "Run it, and see if it works!"

I won't presume to tell you just how to go about teaching your particular group of children, but I would like to share some of my successful ideas, and some of my failures. These are the things which have worked, or not worked, with every group of children I've taught in the past few years.

One word from someone who's been there: book some computer time for yourself during each week, before you start teaching the children. Once they've had a few lessons, they'll insist you stand in line like everyone else!

GENERAL HINTS

If you have no previous experience with the IBM PC, before you do anything else, read through the manual which comes with the machine. It is especially important to understand the directions for setting up the machine, and the safety precautions. To gain an overview of this book, you may wish to study the glossary at the back of the children's section for the most important statements and commands.

The lessons and programs in this book have been aimed at the entry-level IBM PC, a machine with 16K RAM (Random Access Memory). The lessons do not ask the child to load a program from a cassette recorder or a disk drive — the programs are short enough that they can be retyped each time the student wants to try them. In order to use all of the graphics programs in Section 8 and 9, the PC must have a Graphics Adapter installed. Every other program (including "Pine Tree" and "Guess My Number" in Section 9) will run on any monitor or television screen which can display images from the PC.

This book can also be used with the IBM PC-XT and should also be applicable to future IBM personal computer products as well as to the many PC "clones" from other manufacturers which use MS-DOS, the generic equivalent of IBM's PC-DOS. Bear in mind, though, that most of the clones do not have BASIC built-in to the machine and will require the language to be loaded from a disk, a skill not covered in this book. You should be able to teach elementary disk drive operations to a child, though — just be sure to maintain back-ups to your system disks so that important files are not accidentally erased or altered.

The statements and commands used in programs are the most elementary forms of the PC's BASIC. For example, it is true that it is not necessary to use the phase "LET" with the IBM (the computer assumes that a statement like: 35 X = 20 means LET X = 20). But using LET may help the child understand the theory of programming. Also not included in this book are programming conveniences of the PC such as automatic line numbering, program line editing and the Alt key statement and command shortcuts.

SETTING UP YOUR "COMPUTER CENTER": Since programmers tend to get excited and vocal, I suggest that you locate your computer in a semi-secluded area which is near someone in your school who understands the machine. If the children have any problems with the computer, they are going to come and find you anyway, and it's easier if they don't have to call you down the hall from another room.

Secure the electrical cords in a way that keeps them out of the traffic pattern around the computer. Stepping on the cords may cause a fire hazard and will create fuzz on the TV screen.

I schedule only two children at the computer during one time slot. They usually help each other if they encounter difficulties. More than two children at one time may encourage fighting over who will do the typing.

Have enough room for several chairs around the keyboard, and consider where you will place the computer when you teach a group. Sometimes I have used a kitchen timer to keep the children moving, and other times I have run the schedule by the clock. It depends on your group. You will keep your sanity longer if you enforce the rule: "When your turn is over, it's OVER."

A computer notebook for each child is a must. They should learn to take notes on how to do things, or they will never become confident programmers. Discourage them from running to you for answers they should have in their notes.

You may wonder why I have so few sample programs in this book. I have found that the more timid programmers will never pull away from the safety of typing in my programs every time they are on the machine, unless I provide very few samples, and force them to think up their own.

It sounds, from the tone of these hints, that I have many problems with children who program. That isn't the case at all. However, a seemingly trivial problem can eat up precious time when 50 children are waiting to use one computer.

The most important thing you as the teacher must do is to give the children an overall view of the problem you are trying to program. They must see that a problem can be broken down into sections, and each section can be accomplished on the computer in several different ways. Teaching only what a statement does, without focusing on why you would want to use it, creates frustrations for most children.

MY BIGGEST FAILURE OF ALL TIME . . . I can't emphasize this one enough. **DON'T EVER LET YOUR CHILDREN PLAY COMMERCIAL GAME TAPES UNTIL THEY ARE ACCOMPLISHED PROGRAMMERS!!!** By 'accomplished,' I mean the end of the first year for most children.

Let's face it — playing 'Breakout' or 'Computer Hockey' is much more fun, and a lot less work, than learning to program. Especially for elementary school children. If they discover that they can play game tapes on the school computer, they will lose all interest in doing the work involved in learning to program. This is a sad but true fact, and one I learned the hard way. Even with your 12-year-olds, you will regret the day you ever brought a game tape into your computer center. Overnight, they will change from being thrilled about having the chance to try their own programs, to being disappointed because their favorite game tape has been retired. Certainly, they'll have a chance to play games on the computer. But the games should be those that they have written themselves.

GROUP INSTRUCTION: Choose for your computer center a room which has effective shades on the windows. When I teach a group, I place the TV facing them, and I sit at an angle to the keyboard. We talk over what we want to accomplish, and I do the typing. Unless you have a crackerjack typist in the group, it makes lessons unbearably slow if the whole class has to wait while someone hunts and pecks on the keys.

SUGGESTED LESSON OUTLINE—once a week lessons.

Do not go on to the next topic until all the children have had a chance to try out their last lesson on the computer, or they will never remember it. A weekly schedule is imperative for assuring individual children their time at the computer. These lessons follow the sequence of the book:

SECTION 1
1. What is a computer?

SECTION 2
2. Introduce flowcharting
3. Practice writing flowcharts
4. More practice on flowcharts

SECTION 3
5. Running the machine itself, behavior guidelines, and scheduling

SECTION 4
6. Beginning programming: CLS, NEW, LIST, RUN with PRINT examples

SECTION 5
7. PRINT statements with quotation marks, error messages
8. PRINT to skip lines; editing
9. PRINT with arithmetics (+, -, *, /)
10. PRINT variables—simple
11. PRINT variables—such as PRINT A + B

SECTION 6
12. GOTO
13. INPUT
14. RND

SECTION 7
15. FOR-NEXT with PRINT and arithmetic statements
16. More work on FOR-NEXT
17. IF-THEN test
18. IF-THEN in more complex programs (draw flowchart of program function)

SECTION 8
19. Discussion of PSET (X,Y) and plotting of coordinates on paper
20. Graphics worksheets
21. Graphics-make their own initials with PSET
22. Graphics-vertical and horizontal lines
23. More complex programs

SECTION 9
24. Discuss possibilities for designing and carrying out their own programs

TEACHING SUGGESTIONS FOR EACH SECTION

Section 1: What is a computer?

Comparisons to home computer games are helpful. Most children think computers are "smart," and younger children will think they are "magic." Don't overexplain — make arrangements to get the children at the machine as soon as feasible. None of your explanations will really make sense until then.

Section 2: Flowcharting

The objective is logical thinking, not perfection. Have fun! Choose "How To" type topics, which have built-in choices. They must be about something the children understand.

How to: Make pizza; Build a doghouse;
Give a dog a bath; Lose your allowance;
Make a phone call to Grandma.

Set a minimum number of do-loops or branches. I usually set a minimum of three. Use drawing paper. Have the children write the words first, then draw the boxes around the words. It's easier!

Section 4: Getting ready to program

Written quizzes on the meaning of the commands and statements accomplish very little. Let the children learn about this while they type in their own programs. If they don't know what they're doing, their program simply won't run.

The statement CLS at the beginning of each program prevents a great many problems that can arise when many people use the same computer.

Teach the difference between commands and statements. If they do not understand this difference, the children will be frustrated the first few times they work at the computer.

Section 5: PRINT and variables

At the back of the book, you will find samples of PRINT worksheets. This is one of the few areas in which worksheets are of real value.

Discourge the children from using the letter "O" as a variable. It tends to be confusing.

You may delete a line only if you are at the end of the listing of your program. This means that if you have a long program which fills the screen several times when you LIST it, you cannot delete a line until it has scrolled all the way to the end.

I use only variables of one letter with beginning programmers.

Section 6: GOTO, INPUT, RND

Every PRINT line moves the cursor down to the next line. This problem will come up when you teach FOR-NEXT loops with several PRINT statements in the middle.

Look up the use of the semi-colon in the IBM PC manual. Someone will ask you sooner or later how to make things PRINT right next to each other on the same line, using several PRINT statements.

RND is great for visually showing a random distribution when you teach probability.

Section 7: IF-THEN and FOR-NEXT

Reminder: variables must match on FOR-NEXT loops.

The children will have trouble remembering that the computer drops down to the next line if the test is not met in an IF-THEN statement.

Flowcharts may be helpful in tracing the functions of loops and branches in more complex programs. Don't get overly concerned with detail when you draw them.

"X is not equal to Y" is written as X < >Y

Section 8: Graphics programs

The "over and down" motion of plotting a graphics point on the coordinates is similar to drawing a large "7" on the screen.

I have included sample worksheets for practicing coordinates in the back of this section. This is very helpful, especially for the younger children.

When the children number the squares of their graph paper, have them put an 'X' in the upper left-hand corner square. This helps prevent mistakes in numbering.

X	1	2	3	4	5
1	1	2	3	4	5
2	2	6	6	8	10
3	3	6	9	12	5

Tracing the RAIN program through its memory changes is helpful for showing how the values of variables change in the program.

When using variables for the coordinates, I teach the children to use X for horizontal and Y for vertical, at all times. This simplifies things, and prepares the children, in a minor way, for Cartesian Coordinates in mathematics.

Section 9: Sample programs

As stated earlier, with the more timid programmers, I find that too many examples inhibit experimentation.

Section 10: Glossary

I put line numbers in front of all the statements in the examples, to distinguish them from commands.

55